# The Gender Gap In Schools

## Girls Losing Out

*Other titles in the Issues in Focus series:*

# The Gender Gap In Schools

## Girls Losing Out

Trudy J. Hanmer

—Issues in Focus—

ENSLOW PUBLISHERS, INC.
44 Fadem Road          P.O. Box 38
Box 699                Aldershot
Springfield, N.J. 07081   Hants GU12 6BP
U.S.A.                 U.K.

*For Tasia*

**Library of Congress Cataloging-in-Publication Data**

Hanmer, Trudy J.
    The gender gap in schools: girls losing out / Trudy J. Hanmer.
        p. cm. — (Issues in focus)
    Includes bibliographical references and index.
    ISBN 0-89490-718-2
      1. Sex discrimination in education—United States—Juvenile literature.
    2. Women—Education—United States—Juvenile literature. 3. Sex differences
in education—United States—Juvenile literature. I. Title. II. Series: Issues in
focus (Hillside, N.J.)
    LC212.82.H36 1996
    376'.973–dc20                    95-43831
                                                    CIP
                                                     AC

Photo research by Nancy Oakes.

**Illustration Credits:** A. Blake Gardner for Emma Willard School, pp. 14,
16, 19, 25, 30, 48, 57, 62, 83; Courtesy of Emma Willard Archives, pp. 68,
70, 72; Courtesy of Emma Willard School, pp. 22, 34, 42, 91; Courtesy of
Plainfield, New Jersey, Board of Education, p. 53; Courtesy of
Representative Patricia Schroeder, p. 81; Courtesy of Wellesley College
Archives, pp. 75, 77.

**Cover Illustration:** Michael Newman/PhotoEdit.

# Contents

# 1

# "Nothing Lucky About Being a Girl"

At a middle school in San Francisco, a group of seventh and eighth grade girls were asked to describe what was good about being female.[1] Many had discouraging answers, but none was as bleak as fourteen-year-old Marta, who replied, "There's nothing lucky about being a girl. I wish I was a boy."[2]

Marta is not alone. Before dismissing her as a hopelessly negative and unhappy person, consider the results of a recent national survey of three thousand girls and boys. The survey found that girls' self-esteem dropped sharply between elementary school and high school. Far more boys than girls agreed with these phrases: "I like the way I look"; "I like most things about myself"; "I'm happy the way I am." Many more girls than boys agreed with these sentences: "Sometimes I don't like myself that much"; "I wish I were someone else."[3] Clearly, Marta is not the only girl who is discouraged about herself.

To understand why Marta and other girls may feel negative about themselves because of their gender, consider these facts:

- In 1992, girls in the United States received an average weekly allowance of $7.66; boys received an average allowance of $8.87.

- In 1992, the average salary for a female attorney was 75 percent of the average salary for a male attorney.

- Numerous studies of classrooms have shown that girls are called on far less often than are boys and that their answers are listened to far less seriously.

- In a 1990 study of right-to-die cases, it was found that the courts are far less likely to respect a woman's wishes regarding life support than they are to respect a man's wishes; the courts' opinions reflected a widely held belief that women are less capable of making rational decisions than are men.

- If a Barbie doll were a real woman five feet five inches tall, her measurements would be 38-17-28.

- Fifty percent of all nine-year-old girls have been on a diet.

- Fashion models in the United States weigh 23 percent less than the average woman. This means that models, on average, are thinner than 95 percent of all girls and women, even though they are presented as the norm for all women.

- Among high school seniors in 1991, 26 percent of the boys and 14 percent of the girls took physics.

- In 1991, it was reported that women represented only 8 percent of the country's engineers and 16 percent of the employed scientists.

- One out of ten teenage girls in the United States will become pregnant; two thirds of adolescent mothers are single parents.

- Seventy percent of single white mothers and 80 percent of single black mothers are raising their children below the poverty line.

- In a recent study, it was found that nearly 40 percent of all the girls surveyed had experienced some form of sexual harassment by the sixth grade.

- Violence against women is chronic in the United States; every year, almost four million women are beaten by their male partners.

## The Gender Gap

This list presents a number of stark statistics about the lives of girls and women in the United States. Taken together, they present a picture of being female in America that is neither happy nor productive. The patterns of girls' lives apparently become the patterns of women's lives, and too often these are patterns of second-class citizenship. The difference between the achievements of boys and girls and the attainments of men and women have been labeled a "gender gap." In too many areas—education, careers, earning power, self-esteem, productivity, and a number of important safety and health issues—research shows that girls and women are losing out.

Only recently have researchers begun to identify and examine the underlying reasons why this gender gap appears to pervade our society. More and more educators, psychologists, sociologists, scientists, parents, government officials—and girls themselves—are identifying ways in which boys have an edge in society, from elementary school right on through to their position in the workforce.

## Title IX

More than twenty years ago, the United States Congress passed a groundbreaking law that has come to be called Title IX. Title IX was inspired by the civil rights movement of the 1950s and 1960s. The bill was intended to provide equality for girls and women and to end sex discrimination in schools and in the workplace. To most people, it seems that the law has worked.

In the years since this legislation was passed, women have made a number of important gains that seem to indicate growing equality. In recent years, there have been more girls than boys enrolled in college at both the undergraduate and the graduate level. Girls are no longer routinely limited to careers as secretaries, nurses, teachers, wives, and mothers.

In spite of these important gains, there are still areas where inequalities remain, and in some cases even are growing. The average woman with a college degree earns the same as a man with a high school diploma. That means that women must work harder and stay in school longer to earn the same money as do men. Overall, women make only seventy-three cents for every dollar earned by men with equal educations.

The difference is most dramatic in the technical fields related to mathematics and science, where women have yet to make any great gains at all. Work in these fields is typically higher paying and increasingly important as society—and the workforce—become more dependent on technology. Even in scientific areas where girls and women have made remarkable gains, closer analysis still reveals a gap. For example, women now make up 41 percent of medical students, but only 14 percent of the residencies in surgery, long considered the most prestigious—and certainly the most well paid—of the medical specialties. The number of women majoring in engineering fields in college has grown over 100 percent since Title IX was passed, and yet fewer than 10 percent of the nation's engineers are women.

A popular poster neatly summarizes the situation: "Women are 1/2 the world's people; they do 2/3 the world's work; they earn 1/10 the world's income; they own 1/100 of the world's property."

Why this gender gap has developed, why it persists, and what people—including you—can do about it are the subjects of this book.

# 2

## The "Gender Gap"

"[In middle school], no one would speak to me."[1]

These words were said by the recipient of one of the most prestigious awards that any teenager can receive. In 1991, Ashley Reiter was a first-place winner in the Westinghouse Science Talent Search Competition. Westinghouse prizes are awarded for the development of a project in science, mathematics, or technology.

Almost every year, the majority of Westinghouse winners are boys. When Ashley won, her gender was almost as interesting to reporters as her project, which involved mathematical research. Ashley herself had a lot to say about being a girl, about being good in school, and about being smart in mathematics and science. As she recalled in one interview, "I wouldn't even go into the cafeteria for lunch. . . . It was definitely not cool to be smart in seventh and eighth grade, especially for a girl.

Some kids thought they would lose their reputation just by speaking to someone smart."[2] Another teenager echoed Ashley's experience. Rachel Churner remem- bered her seventh grade year as the year she stopped getting good grades. She recalled, "If you were too smart, you would be called a brain. . . . If I got an A and people asked me how I did, I would say, 'I just got a B minus.'"[3]

## Boys' Subjects

Obviously, Ashley found the strength to pursue her academic dreams in spite of the isolation and rejection she experienced, but most people do not. Most people act in ways that will earn them social acceptance by their peer group. For many girls, and for a lot of boys, too, this often means downplaying academic achievement. Especially for girls, being popular means giving up good grades. It means dropping out of classes that are thought of as boys' subjects, such as trigonometry, calculus, physics, and advanced computer science. Decisions about science and math courses are usually made when people are young teenagers. However, they can have lifelong consequences. In college, the vast majority of chemistry, physics, and computer science majors are boys. The numbers are even more startling at higher levels; in 1989, of the nine hundred doctorates awarded in mathematics, only ninety-seven went to women. The pattern continues in the workplace; in 1991, only 8 percent of the engineers in this country were women.

One response to this information might be "So what?" After all, there are other subjects besides mathematics and science and other careers besides

In 1991, women were only 8 percent of the country's engineers and 16 percent of the employed scientists.

engineering. However, a recent national study commissioned by the American Association of University Women found that the better girls feel about their abilities in mathematics and science, the higher their self-esteem, and the greater their aspirations for college and careers, even when they do not become scientists or engineers. In short, the better girls—and boys—feel about their math and science skills, the more confident they feel about their abilities in other areas.

In terms of real earning power, mathematics and science make a difference. A long-term study by the U.S. Department of Education of people who graduated from college in 1972 found that women who earned at least eight credit hours in mathematics in college earned 16 percent more than their peers. For girls who did not go to college, the pattern was the same. Girls who dropped out of high school earned on average $3,000 a year less than male high school dropouts earned. The reason: Girls have taken fewer math and science courses.

## The Worst Year

While working on this book, I asked several adults what their worst year in school had been. Two answers were particularly interesting. Both were from professional people who work in education; one is male and one is female. Both answered, "Seventh grade." Said the woman, "Up until seventh grade, I was really good in math. In fact, I was placed in a gifted and talented program in sixth grade. Then in seventh grade, and I still remember the day, my teacher, Mr. Gillespie, made fun of one of my answers. That was it for me. I stopped

15

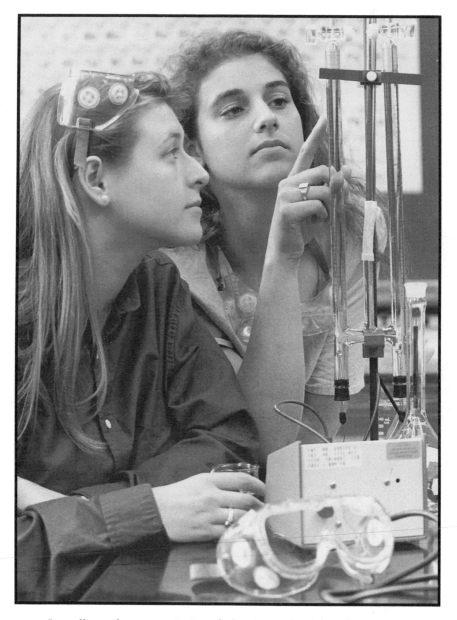

In college, the vast majority of chemistry, physics, and computer science majors are boys.

answering, and pretty soon my math grades went down, and by my junior year in high school, I stopped taking math altogether." When I asked this woman if anything else happened after the incident with Mr. Gillespie, she said, "Sure. After class two of the boys stopped me in the hall and said, 'That was a stupid answer, but it's okay, because girls aren't supposed to have brains, just, you know . . .' and they pointed to my newly developed breasts, and I felt embarrassed and even more humiliated."

Her colleague, a chemistry teacher, also had a lot to say about his physical growth and its impact on his self-esteem in junior high. Remembering his worst year, he said: "Seventh grade . . . yeah, definitely seventh grade. I got pounded all the time in seventh grade. All my friends grew a lot that year, and I was still a skinny little guy. But I showed them. I had a real growth spurt in ninth grade and by my junior year in high school, I could take them all."

For both of these people, seventh grade was obviously a traumatic year. For the man, the ultimate resolution was a successful one. For the woman, on the other hand, the end result was not as satisfying. These are not isolated cases. Increasingly, researchers are turning their attention to the gender gap in society. They are finding that in middle schools and junior high schools across the country, the experience of boys and girls is dramatically different. As Annie Rogers, a Harvard professor who has studied young women's psychological development, has noted, "Girls ages twelve to thirteen no longer know what they knew. They doubt the

17

grounds of their own perception. They question themselves."[4]

Judy Mann, a reporter who researched girls in several middle schools, concluded, "[Seventh grade] is the most dangerous year of a girl's life."[5] She found that experiences in junior high or middle school often set patterns that can account for differences in men's and women's status in society, their career choices, and their earning power.

Kate, a junior in high school looking back on seventh grade, concluded that her experience was terrible, but that she wasn't as aware of it then as she is now. She remembered a male math teacher who told dirty jokes and made sexual comments to the boys about the girls in the class. Like other popular girls in the class, she laughed at the jokes even when they made her uncomfortable; she learned to be silent when women were being ridiculed. No one spoke up against the teacher, because, after all, it was a person in authority telling the jokes. Kate began to feel that maybe girls really were inferior and existed for the amusement of boys.

Anna, another seventh grader, wanted to be an actress and was thrilled to be accepted into an experimental theater group in her hometown. When the group performed a powerful play about sexual harassment, Anna found that many of her junior high classmates did not think the message of the play was important, and some even called her a man-hater. Anna felt isolated and alone except when she was with her older friends from the theater group; when she was ready for high school, she chose to go away to boarding school.

Yet another high school student, Alicia, reflecting on

Many girls find their junior high years to be difficult ones. When girls feel that they are being taken seriously, they feel more confident.

her junior high years, reminisced: "In my small-town public junior high, I was always at the top of my class. The rest of the class made fun of me, calling me names like Dictionary and Encyclopedia because I had such a big vocabulary. I was often ashamed of myself, and would purposely not answer in class."

Finally, there is Laura, who says proudly, "I am smart." During her middle school years, however, she was the subject of her classmates' jokes. Now a college sophomore, she still remembers when "they came at me wielding the poisoned arrows of criticism—'Your handwriting is bad,' 'You wear glasses,' 'You don't like Barbie dolls.' In fifth grade, my name was actually used as a one-word accusation of terminal geekiness. Their accusations began seeping into my veins, and insecurity grew in me because I believed them."

In junior high, more than at any other time in most people's lives, popularity is all-important. When one researcher asked a group of students to draw a scientist, an overwhelming majority of both boys and girls drew pictures of men. Even more important, though, the men they drew were portrayed as unattractive, wild-eyed, nerdy, or crazed. Clearly, this is not the image that a popular junior high girl would want to have of herself. As one teenage girl said, "Being good in science is a weird thing."[6] Being "weird" is not the thing that will insure popularity. Cheerleaders, not scientists, are typically the most popular girls in a school. The criteria for choosing members of cheering squads are usually poise, personality, and appearance. Weird is the opposite of these traits.

## Self-Esteem

Self-esteem is a difficult thing to measure. Psychologists, educators, and parents, as well as young people, know that self-esteem is important, and they know that for most of us self-esteem is most likely to be undermined during adolescence. If the way a person acts, looks, thinks, and believes is not validated by experiences at school, at home, in the community, or in social situations, the person loses self-esteem. Researcher Peggy Orenstein summarizes the work of several psychologists in her definition of self-esteem. Self-esteem is derived from two sources: how a person views her performance in areas in which success is important to her, and how she believes she is perceived by people who are significant in her life, such as parents, teachers, and peers.[7]

The issue of self-esteem permeates discussions of the gender gap. One of the most critical influences on self-esteem is appearance, specifically size and weight. As girls and boys leave childhood and enter adolescence, their bodies undergo a number of physical changes. Growing up means getting bigger. For boys, this natural growth means additional strength that carries with it a physical authority. A boy who is tall and strong can enter a room and know that by his very size he will command attention and respect. For girls, normal growth means gaining weight in their breasts and hips. The average boy is several inches taller than the average girl.

Throughout elementary school, boys and girls are roughly the same size and shape. The changes that take place during adolescence signal different roles and different positions in society. The girls' bodies are now

During elementary school, boys and girls are roughly the same size and shape. The changes that take place during adolescence signal different roles and different positions in society.

more vulnerable to unwanted sexual attention and sexual attack. Boys are now less vulnerable, more in command. The physical differences affect differences in self-esteem. Girls who mature early tend to feel worse about themselves; boys who mature early tend to have higher opinions of their self-worth. The biological differences are very similar; in both cases, bodies are maturing. However, society and culture have attached different values to the development experienced by each sex. For boys, the values are overwhelmingly positive. For girls, they are too often negative.

In terms of physical development, female and male fetuses are the same for the first several weeks, and then the fetuses that undergo the changes necessary to become male babies become physically more vulnerable. Until the sixth week of development, all fetuses, male and female, have the same chromosomal makeup. At that point, in order to become male, some fetuses develop additional hormones. This physical change is apparently fraught with hazards. Male fetuses are less likely to survive and to be born healthy. Female babies are more likely to be skeletally and behaviorally advanced. More girl babies than boy babies survive the traumatic passage from the womb to the world.

## Looking in the Mirror

At puberty, while young women are experiencing body changes within themselves and among their friends, the media—especially magazines, television, and movies—present the ideal young woman as thinner than average. Models weigh 23 percent less than the average woman, and yet their very name—models—indicates that they are the standard to be emulated. The normal adolescent, gaining in the body fat that her body needs for healthy menstruation and successful childbearing later on, suffers in self-esteem because her own physique is not affirmed by what she sees as society's physical standard. One seventh grader, Lisa, poignantly described what being fat did to her self-esteem: "At first I thought if I got good grades and tried to fit in it wouldn't matter how I looked. But I still got teased; it didn't make a difference. All the good things about me—like that I was smart—it was just, 'You don't fit. You don't look good. You're fat.' I felt like I was doing all the good things for no reason. . . . And I don't try at all anymore, I don't care about school."[8]

## Eating Disorders

For Lisa, being fat damaged her self-esteem, which in turn damaged her academic aspirations. For other girls, concern about weight can be even more serious and even life-threatening. While dieting pervades female lives from elementary school on, some girls take weight control to an extreme. It is estimated that at least 4 percent of all teenagers suffer from anorexia nervosa or bulimia nervosa. Anorexia is a medical disorder in which a young person—most likely a girl—starves herself. Girls suffering from bulimia eat excessive amounts of food and then induce vomiting. Fifteen percent of teenage girls, while not technically anorectic or bulimic, practice extreme dieting, induce vomiting, take diet pills, or use laxatives or diuretics to lose weight. By fourth grade, many girls fear being fat or are unhappy about their

Body image becomes increasingly important during adolescence. When girls' minds are taken seriously, they are less likely to be adversely affected by media images of women's beauty.

weight. In a survey of two thousand normal-weight teenage girls, 69 percent were found to be concerned about their weight, and 40 percent were actively dieting.

The medical definition of anorexia is body weight that falls 15 percent below normal. One study showed that 60 percent of Miss America contestants have body weights that are 15 percent below normal, yet who is Miss America? She is the ideal American woman, celebrated as the pinnacle of female physical perfection. If girls can become perfect only by destroying themselves, then we should be glad that most girls' reactions to this impossible ideal is only a loss of self-esteem. Ten percent of girls who try to be physically perfect suffer loss of health, and, in extreme cases of anorexia, such as that of Olympic gymnast Christy Henrich, loss of life. What is perhaps more compelling evidence of society's obsession with thinness in girls is not Miss America, but a study that was done of textbooks used in schools between 1900 and 1980. During that time, the pictures of boys remained the same in terms of size. Girls, on the other hand, were pictured as becoming thinner and thinner with each generation.

Some researchers believe that anorexia is tied to girls' feelings of low self-esteem, to the feeling that they are unimportant. A girl in a science class reported that "the teacher never calls on me, and I feel like I don't exist. The other night I had a dream that I vanished."[9] When the feelings of unimportance become too strong, girls like this may choose to "vanish" through anorexia. Therapists who work with anorectic girls have found another reason for their condition: In a world that they perceive as uncontrollable, the weight of their own bodies becomes the one thing they can control.

## Sexual Harassment

Closely tied to body image is the issue of sexual harassment. Until the 1980s, it was widely assumed that sexual harassment was an adult issue. Few people believed that children were either perpetrators of or victims of sexual harassment involving other children. The U.S. Equal Employment Opportunity Commission has defined sexual harassment as consisting of:

> sexual advances, requests for sexual favors, and other inappropriate verbal or physical conduct of a sexual nature (student to student . . .) when:
> 1) submission to such conduct is made either explicitly or implicitly a term or condition of an individual's employment or education, or when 2) submission to or rejection of such conduct by an individual is used as the basis for academic or employment decisions affecting that individual, or when 3) such conduct has the purpose or effect of substantially interfering with an individual's academic or professional performance or 4) creating an intimidating, hostile, or offensive employment or educational environment.[10]

Most people have understood for a long time that it is wrong for an employer or teacher to use his or her position of power to sexually harass an employee or student. Too few educators and parents, however, have realized the impact on self-esteem that comes from creating a hostile environment, particularly in schools. As girls mature in junior high, it is far too common for them to become objects of sexual taunts and unwanted

27

touching. In 1980, the Massachusetts Department of Education commissioned the first study of sexual harassment in schools. It found that by sixth grade, 42 percent of African-American girls, 40 percent of Hispanic girls, and 31 percent of white girls reported having been harassed.

In 1993, a study of sixteen thousand students in the eighth through eleventh grades found that 85 percent of the girls said they had been sexually harassed. In a survey published in *Seventeen* magazine the same year, 39 percent of the girls aged nine to nineteen said they "had been the target of sexual comments or looks, or had been touched, pinched or grabbed on a daily basis."[11]

While most teachers would interfere if a boy grabbed a girl's breasts, few teachers have been concerned about locker room graffiti about girls' body parts and alleged sexual activities. Girls report that this kind of language and attitude are deeply disturbing and create a hostile atmosphere that makes learning difficult. When adults do little to correct these behaviors, girls' self-esteem is again lowered. They feel that the adults, by their silence, are agreeing with the boys that there is something unclean, unnatural, or shameful about the changes that puberty brings to their bodies.

Fortunately, these attitudes are changing. In several landmark cases, courts have ordered schools to pay damages to girls who were sexually harassed. In a California court, a junior high school was fined $20,000 for not stopping boys from jeering at one of their classmates, Tawnya Brawdy, because of the size of her breasts. In Minnesota, a school was ordered to pay a fine for not erasing graffiti about a female student from the wall of the boys' bathroom.

Without this kind of legal support, girls will have trouble changing boys' behavior. Society has long tolerated explicit sexual remarks by boys toward girls as being natural. After all, "boys will be boys." As one boy said, "No one feels insulted by it. That's stupid. We just play around. I think sexual harassment is normal."[12] Another male junior high student, found guilty of sexual harassment under a new California statute, said, "All the guys do that stuff; it's no big deal. The girls don't mind."[13]

Sexual harassment is indeed a big deal, and girls do mind. Eve Bruneau is a teenager who is pursuing a sexual harassment case in New York State. She alleges that her sixth grade teacher allowed boys to snap girls' bra straps, grab their breasts, and call them derogatory names. Eve remembers, "I dreaded going to school because I couldn't concentrate."[14] An atmosphere that allows the members of one sex the freedom to make disparaging remarks about the members of the other sex adds to feelings of low self-worth.

## Scientific Thinking

Over the past few years, the judges of the Westinghouse Science Talent Search contest have noticed that the projects are increasingly practical. Among the semifinalist proposals for the 1995 contest were plans to develop a wallet for the blind that would allow people who cannot see to keep track of their money. Another project would help with recycling municipal waste, and yet another provided a method for reducing deaths and severe injuries in skiing accidents. In all of these cases,

Girls who compete for the prestigious Westinghouse prize in science
are increasingly interested in projects that will help humanity.

intelligence, coupled with mathematical and scientific knowledge and skill, is directed at improvements in people's lives.

Seventeen-year-old Tracy Phillips designed her "talking wallet" because she had a little brother who was blind. She wanted to study science in order to do "humanitarian projects . . . nothing destructive, like military planes. Science [is] creative and imaginative! It takes human compassion to think of finding the cure for cancer."[15] If half the population—girls—are excluded from the scientific process because their experience excludes them from areas of achievement, all of society will suffer. The gender gap is not just about girls; it is about humanity. Everyone will be more productive in a society where everyone is valued, everyone's talents are challenged, and everyone's achievements are applauded—regardless of whether they are boys or girls, men or women.

Westinghouse winners are, of course, a very small percentage of the population. Until recently, female Westinghouse winners were rarer still. The number of female Westinghouse winners has been increasing however. In terms of gender, one of the most important characteristics of the Westinghouse competition is that the winners are chosen on the basis of projects. In most academic competitions in this country, however, winners are chosen on the basis of standardized tests.

## Crucial Standardized Tests

Teenagers of varying backgrounds and levels of achievement are measured for college, for scholarships,

31

for admission to special programs, and for vocational programs on the basis of test scores. One of the clearest signals that a true gender gap exists in our society is the difference between boys and girls on standardized tests.

Each year, more than a million high school juniors take the Preliminary Scholastic Aptitude Test. The scores on this test are the single most important criterion for determining which students will be named as National Merit Semi-Finalists in their senior year. Being designated as a semifinalist is not only a great honor, it also can be a critical factor in gaining admission to the nation's most selective colleges. For the winners, it is the route of access to millions of dollars in scholarship money distributed by the National Merit Corporation each year. This money comes from more than three hundred businesses and corporations that are interested in encouraging bright young people to attend college, as a way of strengthening America's workforce.

Each year for the past decade, the majority of the test-taking juniors have been girls, but each year among the winning semifinalists, boys outnumber girls by about two to one. For many years, the Educational Testing Service, the organization that is responsible for designing the PSAT, the SAT-I, the SAT-II (a series of tests in different high school subject areas), and a host of other tests, including those used for medical school, law school, and business school entrance, has been concerned about the differences in standardized test scores among a variety of ethnic groups. Native Americans, African Americans, and Hispanic Americans routinely score well below their white schoolmates.

## The Gender Gap in Tests

As alarming as these differences are, it is perhaps even more startling to note that within every ethnic group, girls score lower than do boys. Native American girls, on average, score forty-six points below Native American boys on the SAT. Girls whose families are Hispanic score sixty-two points lower than boys who share the same background. For African-American girls, the gap is smallest (nineteen points), but is perhaps accounted for by the disturbing fact that African-American boys are the most likely to have dropped out of high school without taking the SAT. The fact remains that on the SAT, girls, regardless of their background, do not do as well as boys. The difference is more pronounced in mathematics, but on the verbal section of the test as well as the mathematics section, boys routinely and significantly outscore girls.

It would be outrageous if educators or test developers were to suggest that African Americans or Hispanics score lower than do white students because of differences in their natural aptitudes, and, in fact, no respected educator has suggested such a thing. Instead, millions of dollars have been spent to examine the educational disadvantages that many groups in our society—particularly minority groups—have faced and to adjust the test to meet the educational experiences of different groups. Furthermore, college admissions offices are frank about their willingness to weigh test scores differently for students from different backgrounds.

The National Merit Corporation has instituted separate competitions for students who are Hispanic and

There is a wide gap between girls and boys on the mathematical portions of standardized tests. Some research indicates that boys' experience with toys such as blocks helps with the development of spacial relations and other math skills.

African American in order to address the imbalance in their awards, yet nothing of a similar nature has been done to address the gender differences in test scores. As a leading educational researcher, Myra Sadker, has pointed out, sex discrimination is "the only socially acceptable form of discrimination."[16] Parents who would never suggest that blacks or Hispanics or Native Americans "just can't do math" too often are comfortable consoling their daughters about a low score by saying, "That's okay. Girls aren't good at math."

The gap in test scores is not limited to the SAT. In 1992, on the SAT-II Subject Tests (until recently called the Achievement Tests), boys outscored girls in eleven out of fourteen subjects. In the German, English Composition, and English Literature tests, girls outscored boys, but by very slight differences (three points out of a possible eight hundred on the first two, and six points on the literature test), but in everything else, boys outscored girls. The gap was greatest in physics, where the boys scored sixty-two points more than did the girls. In the European History, Chemistry, Biology, Mathematics I and II, Latin, and American History tests, the boys' scores averaged twenty-five or more points higher than the girls' scores.

At every age the gap remains, and there is evidence that suggests that it grows as students get older. Junior high school students who are particularly gifted can be identified by their schools for participation in the Johns Hopkins Talent Search. Each year, thousands of middle school students take the SAT in the hope of earning entrance into prestigious summer programs sponsored by the Center for Talented Youth. In 1992, among the winners there were nearly six thousand boys and slightly more than forty-five hundred girls. To gain admission to graduate school, college students take the Graduate Record Examination, a more difficult version of the SAT. The gap between men and women on the GRE in 1988 was even greater than the gap between girls and boys on the SAT. On average, women scored one hundred and twenty-seven points lower than men.

Some people have suggested that the gap might reflect girls' and boys' performance in school. Actually, girls generally have higher grades than boys, and among the highest achieving students (those, for example, who are likely to be National Merit Semi-Finalists), the gap is even greater. One pair of researchers has found that a girl with an A+ average typically scores eighty-three points lower on the SAT than a boy with an A+ average. For college students applying to law school, again a typically high-achieving group, the pattern is the same. Women and men with the same GPA (grade point average) in their classes do not have the same chance of being admitted to the law school of their choice or of receiving financial assistance that is most often based, at least partially, on standardized testing. Women are statistically likely to score lower than their male classmates on the LSAT, the standardized test used for law school admission.

The gap is not confined to standardized tests that are used for college and graduate school. In New York City public schools in 1994, school officials found that a gender gap existed on reading and mathematics tests given to all students in grades two through ten. In a pattern that matches that found with college and graduate school tests, "the scores revealed a gender gap that grows as boys and girls get older."[17] The gap existed on both the reading and the mathematics tests, although it was somewhat more pronounced in math. An analysis of the scores showed that in spite of the fact that girls and boys start out with even test results, "girls tended not to perform as well as their male counterparts by the higher grades."[18] As Myra and David Sadker have concluded, "Females are the only group in America to begin school testing ahead and leave having fallen behind."[19] In fact, during adolescence both boys and girls show a decline in IQ test scores, but the drop for boys is only three points, while the drop for girls is thirteen points.

Do standardized test scores really matter all that much? Most students would answer with a resounding yes. They might answer yes because they understand the connection between high achievement on standardized tests and admission to college, access to financial aid, or entry into certain prestigious professions. It is more likely that their answer would be based on something far more personal—their feelings of self-esteem and how those feelings are influenced by test scores. Put another way, "Boys looking into the SAT mirror see in it an image bigger than life. Girls see less than is really there."[20] Researchers have found that SAT scores underpredict how girls will do in college, and they overpredict how boys will do. What that means is that if a boy and a girl have the same SAT scores, the likelihood is that the girl will earn better grades than will the boy.

In light of the ways in which standardized tests are used, it is easy to see how standardized test scores can have a relentless impact on self-esteem. Standardized test scores by their very name are part of the educational process for many adolescents: They are standards. Most people define themselves as normal or abnormal by comparing themselves to whatever is being presented as standard. A girl who is used to doing as well as or better than the boys in her classroom has her faith in her own achievements shaken when they do better than she does on a standardized test.

Sometimes parents contribute to these feelings. I once overheard a father discussing his daughter's SAT scores. She was an intelligent, attractive, musically gifted student who consistently earned Bs in classes that included chemistry, trigonometry, and French IV. His comment: "Nobody will want her with scores like that." In one statement, he managed to wipe out all of her many accomplishments as being less important than her SAT scores. Whether or not she heard him say that, it is likely that she received the message from him in countless subtle ways.

Clearly, this father might have said the same thing about a son with low scores, but the fact remains that many more boys than girls score better than expected. Since the scores are given so much attention, the boys' self-esteem is likely to be enhanced. For a boy, a C in math—perhaps the result of sloppy homework and inattention in class—is more likely to be offset by a high math score on the SAT. This tells him that by the standards that count, he's doing just fine.

In numerous studies around the country over the last decade, boys and girls have been asked what it would be like to switch gender. Invariably, most boys view becoming a girl as negative, while girls view becoming a boy as positive. To be a girl, for most boys, is seen as limiting opportunities. To be a boy, for most girls, is seen as widening opportunities. Two responses from a middle school in San Francisco are typical: A girl replied, "If I were a boy, I'd get to play a lot more sports." Her male classmate's reaction: "If I were a girl, I'd have to stand around at recess instead of getting to play basketball."[21]

What is there in girls' and boys' lives that has made their experiences so different? Since 1980, a host of researchers have worked to find answers to this question.

# 3

# The Search for Reasons

In 1979 when Robert Parker came from Groton School—which had been an all-boys' school for most of its existence—to Emma Willard School, which had always been an all-girls' school, he quickly noticed a dramatic difference. It took the new principal very few months to realize that there were significant differences between the students at his former school and those at his new school in Troy, New York. He was particularly intrigued by the attitude of his students to grades. When he handed back essays, he found that girls tended to frame discussions of low grades around issues of fairness and relationship. That is, they saw a grade as representing whether or not he liked them. He had not had this experience with boys.

Parker hypothesized, or made an assumption, that gender might be the reason for the differences in attitudes between his current female students and his former male students. As is the habit with schoolteachers, he turned to the library to see if he could find some research that would show him how and why girls learn and think. His intuition told him that girls' methods and approaches to learning were different from those of boys. What he found shocked him. In 1980, he could find almost no research that focused on the psychology of healthy adolescent females.

## How Girls and Women Think

What he did find was one magazine article, "Woman's Place in Man's Life Cycle."[1] In this article, Dr. Carol Gilligan, a professor of psychology at the Harvard Graduate School of Education, explained her theory that girls and women use very different methods of decision-making from those employed by boys and men. She argued that psychologists had built their definitions of moral reasoning on models that were more applicable to men's experiences than to women's, and that ways of solving problems and the value systems accepted as absolute, or without doubt, by many in the field of psychology were not always appropriate when applied to girls and women. Dr. Gilligan also suggested that many institutions in western culture—particularly schools, legal systems, and churches—had incorporated this male model of decision-making.

By 1981, Dr. Gilligan had developed her theory more fully in a groundbreaking book, *In a Different Voice*. In this book, she expanded her theory and used it to explain a number of phenomena about girls and

Dr. Carol Gilligan and other researchers have identified major differences in the ways that girls and boys, women and men, make decisions. This may contribute to differences in the development of girls' and boys' leadership skills.

women. For instance, she thought that for girls not to have their value systems and decision-making reflected in the majority of the authoritative institutions in their world led to their silence. Wrote Gilligan, "In novels of education written by women, the astute and outspoken and clear-eyed resister often gets lost in a sudden disjunction or chasm as she approaches adolescence, as if the world that she knows from experience in childhood suddenly comes to an end and divides from the world she is to enter as a young woman, a world that is governed by different rules. . . . As the river of a girl's life flows into the sea of Western culture, she is in danger of drowning or disappearing."[2] Dr. Gilligan also asserted that girls and women put a far greater emphasis and a much higher value on relationships than did boys and men. While boys and men tended to stress individualism and to see independence as a measurement of maturity, she believed that girls were far more likely to measure maturity by the ability to create and sustain relationships. Cooperation, sharing, collaboration, and care and responsibility for others were highly prized by girls and women. On the other hand, separation, individualism, and strict standards of justice were judged as most valuable by men and by the culture at large.

Although Dr. Gilligan had begun to study men's and women's moral development while she was a graduate student at Harvard, she had a new goal in mind in the early 1980s. Psychologists had long agreed that adolescence was a critical time in a person's development. What impact, wondered Dr. Gilligan, would there be on adolescent females if their point of view was not validated? At Emma Willard School, Robert Parker needed

43

answers to questions such as how the girls in his school chose their courses, how they chose their peer leaders, and why their responses to criticism seemed so different from that of the boys he was used to teaching. Dr. Gilligan wanted a group of adolescent females whom she could interview to test her hypotheses.

## The Emma Willard Study of Girls' Values

Robert Parker invited Carol Gilligan to use Emma Willard students for her research. She accepted. From 1981 to 1984, Dr. Gilligan, her colleague Dr. Nona Lyons, and a host of graduate students traveled to the school each year in order to interview a group of randomly selected students. Although the interviews were one and a half to two hours long, there were two questions that were critical. The first one was "How do you describe yourself to yourself?" Next, the students were asked to describe a "moral dilemma," a time when they faced a tough decision and were not quite sure what to do. The interviewers asked not only what decision they made, but what factors they considered in making that decision.

The dilemmas that the girls faced ranged from minor to very serious. One girl told the interviewer that the dilemma she faced was whether or not to tell her mother that her father was getting remarried. Even though her parents were divorced, she knew that "my mother still loved my father a great deal." She concluded that "it was a really hard decision on my part as to whether and when to tell my mother that, because on the one hand, I knew that it was really going to kill her to find out, and on the other hand, I thought I had an obligation to tell her."[3]

For another girl, the dilemma was how to tell her parents about bad grades. She told the interviewer, "I lied to my parents about my grades. I told them that my biology grade was going to be marvelous, and it is not going to be marvelous."[4] For a third girl, a dilemma arose when she wanted to spend the night with a good friend and she couldn't reach her mother to ask permission. Trying to figure out what to do, she weighed her friend's needs and her mother's needs: "I don't think it is just my own selfish reasons, [because] I think it would be good for my friend to have me there when she needs somebody to talk to. . . . And then the other side is I just don't want to do something without Mom's permission."[5]

In all of the issues that these girls raised, a central problem for each of them was how to preserve relationships with parents or with friends. The responsibility for making relationships work became a central force in the decision-making process. According to Gilligan, this was a responsibility that many psychologists had not weighed heavily enough in determining how people make decisions.

The results of the interviews were coded, tabulated, and analyzed. For many years, psychologists had measured adults' moral development (which includes decision-making skills) on a very precise scale that was developed by Dr. Lawrence Kohlberg at Harvard. Dr. Kohlberg had been one of Dr. Gilligan's teachers in graduate school. Although she admired his work, she felt that the scale he used, which he had developed after working exclusively with white males, did not necessarily apply to all human beings and that women, in particular, were poorly served by it. According to Kohlberg's scale, the more adult or mature a person's thinking became, the more that person was willing to use impersonal standards of right and wrong to make a decision, regardless of the human relationships that were involved.

If Dr. Gilligan's hypothesis was right, the preservation of relationships would be more important to most females than an impersonal set of standards about right and wrong. Furthermore, it was clear that a girl's self-esteem would suffer if the standard by which she made decisions—the preservation of relationships—was not the one that she was taught to use by her school, her religion, and her society. This was the hypothesis that Gilligan was testing in her interviews with Emma Willard students. Her coworker, Dr. Lyons, had developed a way of looking at the responses to the interview questions that would enable the researchers to count the number of times that the girls used relationships in their self-descriptions and in their solutions to moral dilemmas. Over the course of the four years that the study was conducted, Dr. Gilligan found that she was right. A large majority of the girls did value relationships as central to their decision-making process. For example, a yearbook editor found herself doing extra work because she didn't want to fire a staff member who was not meeting deadlines, but was a good friend. Another girl, whose roommate had stolen her mathematics book, developed an elaborate scheme for getting it back without actually accusing the girl of stealing, so that she could preserve their roommate relationship.

Dr. Gilligan and Emma Willard School published the results of this study in a book, *Making Connections: The Relational Worlds of Girls at Emma Willard School.* Psychologists, teachers, and parents all over the country read the book. Most of them felt that it contained important information that helped them understand the differences between girls and boys. Critics of the work, on the other hand, felt that boys and girls were more alike than they were different and that pointing out differences that were gender related might provide people with an excuse for not allowing girls equal opportunities. After all, they argued, if a girl is inherently unwilling or unable to use impersonal standards of right and wrong, then maybe women are not suited to become lawyers and judges. On the contrary, replied Gilligan and her supporters, perhaps systems of justice that rest on impersonal standards need to be broadened to reflect the values and experiences of all humanity. Furthermore, Gilligan insisted that girls understood and used standards of justice but preferred to focus on the importance of responsibility in relationships.

## The Jolt of Junior High

As the debate continued, Dr. Gilligan and another colleague, Dr. Lyn Mikel Brown, took their research to all-girls Laurel School in Cleveland, Ohio. Here they hoped to extend the study by listening seriously to younger girls. It had become increasingly apparent to Brown and Gilligan in talking to teachers and parents, that most girls underwent a major transformation around the age of eleven or twelve, just at the time they entered middle school or junior high school. Although

Studying math and science in an all-girls' environment may strengthen girls' achievement and interest in these subjects.

this age coincided with puberty, the onset of puberty was also a factor in boys' development, so they hypothesized that it was not the physical changes themselves that determined the changes in girls.

At Laurel School, which included girls in the seventh and eighth grades, Brown and Gilligan listened to girls who were younger than the Emma Willard high school students. After working with these girls for five years, Brown and Gilligan published their findings in a book, *Meeting at the Crossroads.* They observed that as girls grew older, they became unsure of their opinions.

In a summary of their findings, Brown reflected that the younger girls were outspoken, confident, likely to take risks in relationships, to engage in conflict, to express a wide range of feelings, from joy and pleasure to anger and sadness, and to feel entitled to be heard. She also noted that the two researchers found the girls beginning to take in feminine stereotypes and images of the perfect girl, the girl who has no bad thoughts or feelings, who is always nice and kind, and never mean or bossy. As the girls began to move into adolescence, and their bodies became more like women's bodies, the pressure to adopt and adapt to this image increased, and a real struggle broke out as girls fought against and resisted this pressure. The unresolvable dilemma for girls was whether to stay in touch with their thoughts and feelings and risk being isolated from the wider culture, or to adapt to the stereotypes society held for girls and risk disconnecting from themselves. Low self-esteem was directly connected to trying to be popular; the more they tried to be perfect the more their self-esteem suffered. On the other hand, Brown stressed that some girls resisted, often at the expense of immediate popularity, but without losing their own sense of confidence and self, strengths that would serve them better in the long run.[6]

From their interviews, Brown and Gilligan found that older girls—in this case thirteen- and fourteen-year-olds as opposed to nine- and ten-year-olds, used the phrase "I don't know" frequently. They were tentative in voicing their opinions. Ten-year-olds, by contrast, were sure, outspoken, and did not hesitate to let the interviewers know what they thought. Gilligan and Brown concluded that something happens on a girl's journey from childhood to adulthood. Whatever that something is, in most cases, it is not positive. Many girls do not become stronger, more confident, and more likely to state their opinions. On the contrary, they lose self-esteem, lose faith in their abilities and opinions, and gradually narrow the options they see for themselves. Brown hypothesizes that this happens because of the social expectations and the messages that girls receive, often from well-meaning adults—women as well as men—that urge them to conform to a feminine stereotype. Girls must struggle to remain connected to themselves under this pressure, which has the whole force of the culture behind it. It is not surprising that girls begin to feel uncertain about what they know, about what they really feel, and what they really think.[7]

While many people were interested in Gilligan's early work, to some it seemed too theoretical and abstract. The field of moral psychology is only one small branch of psychology, and Kohlberg's scale hardly influenced the way people conducted their everyday lives.

The research that Gilligan and her colleaques did in schools, however, attracted much notice. Throughout the 1980s and into the 1990s, people who were concerned about the gender gap and about the relationship between experience and self-esteem focused increasingly on school as the place where much of the damage was being done. In a country committed to democratic goals of fair treatment and equality of opportunity, it seemed especially ironic that public schools, founded specifically to foster democratic ideals, would be places where half of the population was treated unequally:

> Teacher: What's the capital of Maryland? Joel?
> Joel: Baltimore.
>
> Teacher: What's the largest city in Maryland, Joel?
> Joel: Baltimore.
> Teacher: That's good. But Baltimore isn't the capital. The capital is also the location of the U.S. Naval Academy. Joel, do you want to try again?
> Joel: Annapolis.
>
> Teacher: Excellent. Anne, what's the capital of Maine?
> Anne: Portland.
>
> Teacher: Judy, do you want to try?
> Judy: Augusta.
> Teacher: Okay.

This dialogue between a teacher and her students was recorded by two of the most important researchers studying behavior in schools, Myra and David Sadker, a husband and wife team. From a 1985 article in *Psychology Today* to their most recent work, *Failing at Fairness,*

51

the Sadkers have tirelessly documented the presence of and consequences of sexism in the classroom. They have assessed hundreds of classrooms from elementary school to high school and they have found that, regardless of whether the teacher is a man or a woman, boys are at an advantage in coeducational classrooms. In many classroom settings, like the one in the dialogue, boys are listened to more seriously, questioned more closely, and taught to feel that whatever they are saying—whether or not they are right or wrong—is taken more seriously and counts more than what girls are saying.

One girl explained what she felt when she sat in her English class: "My teacher asks [a question] . . . I know the answer, but I contemplate whether I should answer the question. The boys in the back are going to tease me like they harass all the other girls in our class. . . . I want to tell them to shut up. But I stand alone. . . . In my ninth period class, I am actually afraid—of what [the boys] might say. . . . As my frustration builds, I promise myself that I will yell back at them. I say that every day . . . and I never do it."[8]

By not calling on girls as often as they do on boys, by not noticing that the bright girls in a classroom are not volunteering answers, and by not correcting the behavior of boys that contributes to girls' reluctance to speak out, teachers create classrooms that are hostile learning environments for girls.

## Sexism in the Classroom

After the passage of federal legislation in 1972 barring sex discrimination in any educational institution receiving federal funds, many people believed that sex

In the 1960s, concern about sex roles in school curricula led schools to offer courses traditionally considered to be girls' subjects to boys, and boys' subjects to girls. These boys, for example, are studying home economics.

discrimination in schools had been wiped out. The Sadkers found, however, that a subtle but pervasive sexism remained in force in many classrooms in the 1980s. Their first extensive study was a three-year project that ended in 1985. During that time, the Sadkers and a team of researchers visited more than a hundred fourth, sixth, and eighth grade classes. The teachers were male and female, black and white, and came from (and worked in) urban, suburban, and rural communities. After observing these classrooms and recording the class discussions that they heard, they concluded that boys call out in class more, that boys receive more praise from teachers than do girls, and that boys are more likely to dominate class discussions. The Sadkers believe that these patterns continue in the workplace; as they wrote, "sexist treatment in the classroom encourages formation of patterns . . . which give men more dominance and power than women in the working world."[9]

In 1994, the Sadkers published *Failing at Fairness,* a comprehensive report on the work they had been doing for more than a decade. They concluded that in 1994, nearly a decade after they first identified the subtle patterns of sexism in the classroom, "today's schoolgirls face subtle and insidious gender lessons, micro-inequities that appear seemingly insignificant when looked at individually, but that have a powerful cumulative impact."[10]

Among other things, they found that textbooks still neglect women, particularly in picturing scientists and mathematicians as mostly male, that male teachers are guilty of subtle and not so subtle sexual harassment such as calling girls by nicknames and inserting slides of women in bikinis into lectures to hold student (that is, male) attention. They found that boys were still being called on more often, questioned more closely, praised more fully, and allowed to dominate the classroom. They found that although girls vie for teacher attention in the elementary grades, as they grow older, they grow quieter. They concluded, "Every day in America little girls lose independence, achievement and self-esteem."[11]

The Sadkers found that race also had an impact on the relationship between teachers and students. White males got the most attention, followed by minority males, white females, and finally minority females. Among minority females, Hispanic females are found to be the least likely to be called on and the least likely to call out in class. The experience of these Latinas provides compelling evidence that the experience of being overlooked in the classroom can have dire consequences. Latinas are also most likely to become mothers as teenagers, most likely to be in gangs, and most likely to drop out of high school. Not surprisingly, they experience the greatest drop in self-esteem during their teenage years.

Perhaps most damaging to girls, because it seems so harmless, is what the Sadkers have identified as the okay response. Teachers tend to reward girls' answers with a bland "Okay" rather than questioning or analyzing their answers. They also tend to do the problems for girls rather than encouraging them to work out problems for themselves. This "kills them with kindness," conclude the Sadkers, and creates a situation where girls "don't learn strategies to get it right [and] will never correct their mistakes."[12]

A boy complained to the Sadkers that "I have found

that teachers will help girls and tell them the answer. If boys don't know the answer, they will be made to solve it themselves."[13] What seems unfair to him now will prove to be a strength later on when he trusts his own judgments and abilities more than will the girls who have been told the answers. A mathematics teacher put it another way when she said, "I know I don't always hold them accountable the same way. I let the girls off the hook because they get so embarrassed when they're wrong."[14] The girls are "off the hook" for the moment, but shortchanged in the long run, because they will not be engaging actively in their educations in the same way that boys do.

## The College Experience

If "the single most valuable resource in a classroom is the teacher's attention,"[15] then girls are impoverished in most of the nation's classrooms. In their report on college and graduate school classes, Bernice Sandler and Roberta Hall found that the patterns of teacher-student interaction documented in elementary and high schools continued at higher levels. They found that professors were more likely to remember men's names, more likely to call on men, and more likely to listen to their answers. In their study they quoted a female Ph.D. candidate at Harvard who commented that she felt that she had entered graduate school on an equal footing with her male colleagues, but "having experienced the discrimination—the refusal of professors to take you seriously; the sexual overtures and the like—you limp

At all levels of education, most mathematics and science teachers are males. Researchers are probing the impact, if any, of this factor on the low numbers of girls majoring in these disciplines.

out doubting your own ability to do very much of anything."[16]

The more advanced the course of study and the more prestigious the institution, the more likely it is that the professors will be male. The lack of role models for female students may add to their discomfort in the classroom. In the early 1990s, professors in engineering were 98 percent male, in natural sciences men accounted for 83 percent of the professors, and in business men held 75 percent of the professorships. Researchers, including the Sadkers, believe that the limited number of women teaching in these fields helps to explain why so few women enter careers in these areas.

It is not only curriculum that determines the gender of the faculty. The more elite the institution, the less likely it is to have female professors. Among Ivy League colleges and universities, only 10 to 13 percent of the tenured faculty positions are held by women, who earn an average of $14,000 a year less than do their male colleagues. In the less distinguished community colleges, women hold nearly half of the faculty positions. Throughout the educational world, then, there are gender patterns that keep women in a second-class position.

## The Influence of Schools

In the early 1990s the American Association of University Women (AAUW) published two reports that focused on these gender patterns in schools. First, it published a study, *How Schools Shortchange Girls,* which analyzed more than thirteen hundred recent studies on girls' development. The AAUW was concerned about the fact that the national debate over education did not address any special concerns of girls, even though the research done during the 1980s clearly indicated that coeducational school settings were not serving many girls well. By summarizing key points of the major research reports from the 1980s, the AAUW hoped to draw national attention to the problem.

The authors of the AAUW report reviewed the thirty-five reports issued on education by the federal government during the 1980s to see whether or not they considered specific gender issues. They found that the only gender-specific problem that was identified was teenage pregnancy (viewed as the teen mother's exclusive problem). Researchers focused on pregnancy because pregnant teens tend to drop out of high school, to be single mothers, and to need welfare. The fact that teenage pregnancy has been linked to the failure of schools to encourage self-esteem in girls, or that girls with learning problems are the most likely to become pregnant and drop out, was ignored in all of the national studies.

In summarizing the areas where gender plays a significant role, *How Schools Shortchange Girls* covered education from preschool to vocational and college preparatory high school programs. The report touched on issues of domestic violence, pregnancy, suicide, eating disorders, and bias in standardized testing. Although they clearly did not hold schools solely responsible for these problems, the researchers did conclude that the educational establishment had not done enough to make schools welcoming places where girls are given their fair share of attention. They concluded, "Students sit in classes that, day in and day out, deliver the message that women's lives count for less than men's."[17] This message may be directly linked to the decline in self-esteem that girls experience during their school years. As the historian Linda Kerber has suggested, "Lowered self-esteem is a perfectly reasonable conclusion if one has been subtly instructed that what people like oneself have done in the world has not been important and is not worth studying."[18]

## The Self-Esteem Gap

In order to document the connection between school experiences and self-esteem, the AAUW commissioned a study in 1990. Researchers conducted a national survey of three thousand boys and girls aged nine to fifteen. Dr. Carol Gilligan, among others, was enlisted to help design the questions that the students were asked. The results were startling. Although boys and girls differed somewhat in self-esteem as young children, the gap grew far wider as they grew older.

For example, in elementary school, 60 percent of the girls and 67 percent of the boys described themselves as "happy the way I am." By high school, 46 percent of the boys but only 29 percent of the girls described themselves this way. Other statements reflecting self-esteem showed the same gap. Many more girls than boys said that they wished they were someone else, and many more boys than girls said that they "like most things about myself."

Interestingly, the study showed that African-American girls did not suffer the loss of self-esteem that white and Hispanic girls suffered. In fact, they began elementary school full of confidence that grew as they grew older. Although these girls retain their self-esteem, they often do so at the expense of their connection to school. They feel good about themselves, but not about themselves in school, so they are more likely to drop out than are white teenagers. If their disconnection from school helps them to maintain their self-esteem, this is yet another reason to question how safe and healthy schools are for girls.

*Shortchanging Girls, Shortchanging America* had as one of its central themes a concern that the United States was not using all of the talent in society because girls were not being fully educated. Among the interview questions were several that dealt with the way boys and girls felt about mathematics and science, critical areas of the school curriculum in an increasingly technological world. The results were consistent with other findings. In these areas, which traditionally were regarded as male domains, girls did not feel confident of their abilities. Although 52 percent of the boys in the study said they would enjoy being scientists, only 29 percent of the girls said they would like a career in a scientific field. While 50 percent of the elementary school boys said they were good at math, only 33 percent of the elementary school girls described themselves as good at this subject. By high school, only 14 percent of the girls described themselves as good at math.

All of the research in the 1980s and early 1990s indicates that schools are not completely fair to girls. Yet for years, Americans have pointed to their public educational system as being one of the outstanding hallmarks of the world's leading democratic system.

By high school only 29 percent of all teenage girls say they would enjoy careers as scientists.

After the advances of the civil rights and women's movements of the 1960s and 1970s, most Americans believed that any vestiges of sex discrimination would be wiped out. Schools have kept this double standard, and the curriculum has contributed to an atmosphere that is less helpful to girls' learning than it is to boys'.

# 4

# Schools: "No Girls Allowed"

From colonial days until the nineteenth century, most Americans did not believe that girls needed to go to school. After all, their role in life was strictly limited. Girls were not expected to have any careers except those of wife and mother. Their education was limited to learning domestic skills—cooking, sewing, child care, and nursing—all of which could be taught at home. Few women shared the vision of Lucy Downing, a colonial woman. In the 1600s she wrote to John Winthrop, the first Governor of Massachusetts Bay and one of the men responsible for the establishment of Harvard College, "I would teach [women] all that men are taught."[1]

Unfortunately for Lucy Downing and for any other colonial woman who had the nerve to suggest that women needed formal education, colonial society was ruled by Christian men who adhered strictly to the New

Testament teachings of Paul. They interpreted his statement "I permit not a woman to teach" to mean that a woman did not need to have access to books; did not need to learn history, science, or mathematics; should not speak outside the home; and should play no role in public affairs.

During most of the seventeenth and eighteenth centuries, in fact, the idea of schooling for women was considered to be so ridiculous that as towns and villages established public schools, they did not even bother to exclude girls. When they used the word "children" instead of "boys" in their charters, some girls used this fact as a way to get into school. One historian of women's education, Elaine Kendall, has discovered that girls who attempted to attend these early colonial schools were kept separate from the boys. They were sometimes allowed to sit on the steps outside the schoolhouse and listen through the windows, or they were allowed to sit in the rear of the school behind a curtain. The conditions for learning were difficult. When girls suffered from colds and lung diseases, natural ailments for children forced to sit in cold or drafty places, the conclusion was drawn that learning made girls sick.[2]

The colonists in the Mid-Atlantic area, particularly the Dutch who settled New York, allowed girls to study with boys in the primary grades. Even here, though, the rule was that "Boys and Girls should be separated as much as possible from each other."[3]

When the colonists threw off British rule during the American Revolution, there was a great deal of rhetoric about freedom. The Declaration of Independence declared that "all men are created equal." While it is probably safe to assume that the vast majority of the American colonists defined "men" as white males, there were those who felt that freedom and liberty, the Revolutionary ideals, should apply to everyone and that the term "men" really meant "mankind" or "humanity." Typical of those who wanted to see American women included equally in the new society was Abigail Adams, who urged her husband, John, to "remember the ladies" when he was writing laws for the new nation. She herself had had no formal education and keenly felt this loss.

By 1788, a new Constitution had been written for the new nation. Like the Declaration of Independence, the constitution used the pronouns "he" and "him" exclusively. Once again, however, the document sparked conversations about liberty and freedom that rightfully could be extended to all citizens. It was generally understood, particularly in the Northern states, that education was one way to safeguard democracy. The New England states were the first to decide that public education was necessary if the citizens (males, of course) of the United States were to be capable of voting intelligently and planning for the industrial growth that coincided with the birth of the new nation. They began to use tax money to set up schools.

In some cases, town leaders set aside money for girls' education as well as for the education of boys. Most often, this meant that girls had to attend school when the boys were not there, because almost everybody believed that it was unhealthy, if not immoral, for boys and girls to study together. Sometimes the girls studied in the early morning before the boys arrived, typically from 5:00 to 7:00 A.M., and sometimes they were permitted to study in the late afternoon or early evening, after the boys were finished for the day. Some towns let the girls have the schoolroom in the summer, when the boys were needed to work in the fields and could not attend school. Many communities, however, specifically excluded girls from school. For example, Wellesley, Massachusetts, which ironically later would be the home of a great women's college, declared in 1792 that its budget would "not [include] any expense for educating girls."[4]

In the first decades of the nineteenth century, the country was swept with a new democratic fervor. The War of 1812 stimulated American industrialism and broke forever the dominance of Europe over the New World. The nation was expanding westward, technology was advancing rapidly, and reform movements were sweeping the country. By 1830, most towns and villages that had schools (the South still relied heavily on home tutoring for boys because of the vast distances between plantations) provided elementary or primary education for girls as well as boys.

## The Beginnings of Education for Women

In one of the most radical acts in support of women's education, a young woman named Emma Hart Willard started a school for "the higher education of young women" in her home in Middlebury, Vermont. As the young wife of an older man, Willard had a nephew who was her own age and who attended Middlebury College, which was not open to women. Emma Hart Willard studied mathematics and science from the textbooks that the nephew brought home and determined that girls

Emma Hart Willard pioneered equal education for girls when she opened a seminary where girls could learn math and science, subjects previously taught only to boys.

could and should learn the same subjects that their brothers did.

The state of Vermont was not friendly to the idea of higher education for women. In order to build the kind of school she envisioned, Emma Hart Willard needed public tax support. Because New York was a more progressive state, in 1818 she appealed to its legislature for funding. Although the state gave her little money, she attracted the attention of the citizens of Troy, New York, a bustling, growing city on the Hudson River. With their help, she was able to purchase a school building and move to Troy, where she opened the Troy Female Seminary in 1821.[5]

In her speech to the legislature (which had to be delivered by a man because women were not allowed to make public addresses), Emma Hart Willard boldly declared, "Our sex too are the legitimate children of the legislature."[6] At the same time, however, she spoke for her generation when she argued that the major reason for educating women was to prepare them to be better wives and mothers:

> Our sex need but be considered in the single relation of mothers. . . . Would we rear the human plant to its perfection, we must first fertilize the soil which produces it. If it acquire its first bent and texture upon a barren plain, it will avail comparatively little, should it afterwards be transplanted to a garden.[7]

The seminary at Troy was a forerunner of a new kind of educational institution that sprang up all over the country in the 1830s. Although some were more rigorous than others in their curriculum, following Emma

TROY FEMALE SEMINARY.

The Troy Female Seminary, founded by Emma Hart Willard, was one of dozens of new schools for girls opened in the nineteenth century. Because seminaries charged tuition, most girls still had no access to higher education as public schools continued to offer boys a more challenging curriculum at no cost.

Hart Willard's example of teaching mathematics and science, all had a few things in common. They were exclusively female, they taught what has been called the "3 M's—morals, mind and manners,"[8] and they began to prepare women for a new career outside the home. Women could now add teaching to the list of acceptable occupations for their sex.

As the movement for public education grew, so did the need for teachers. The seminaries produced the needed labor to staff the growing schools, and women could be paid far less than men. It was assumed that they would teach only until they got married and that they would always have either their fathers or husbands as their main source of financial support.

## The First Women's College

Once women had access to seminary education, they wanted more. The seminaries paved the way for women's colleges. In 1837, Mary Lyon founded a seminary in South Hadley, Massachusetts, that became Mt. Holyoke College, the first women's college in the United States. Oberlin College opened its doors to women in 1833, but the course of study, called the Ladies' Course, was little more than a seminary education. When an outstanding student, Lucy Stone, was asked to prepare the commencement address, she did so knowing that even at Oberlin, she would not be allowed to deliver the speech. Her words would be read by a male student.

Even though they had far fewer opportunities than their white sisters, young black women were beginning

At girls' seminaries in the nineteenth century, young women had access to libraries and faculty that had previously been available only to boys.

to benefit from the seminary system even before the Civil War. The Miner Normal School for Colored Girls, which would become Miner Teachers' College, opened in Washington, D.C., in the 1850s.

Although women were beginning to be educated in schools of their own, coeducation remained a controversial topic. Many women, including Elizabeth Cady Stanton, a great women's rights activist of the nineteenth century, believed that women would never have equal educations to those of their brothers unless they had access to men's colleges and graduate schools. Although she had been educated at the Troy Female Seminary, she argued that women would not be fully educated until they attended school with men. Referring to boy and girl twins, she noted, "If the Creator could risk placing the sexes in such near relations, they might with safety walk on the same campus and pursue the same curriculum."[9]

In the second half of the nineteenth century, women attempted to break down educational barriers with limited success. Elizabeth Blackwell became the first doctor in the United States when she finally gained admission to a medical school in Geneva, New York, but her practice was limited to women and children. Men refused to be treated by a woman.

Most men reached the conclusion that educating women beyond grade school was not only unnecessary, but harmful. When the University of Michigan voted against admitting women in 1858, the president declared, "When we attempt to disturb God's order, we produce monstrosities."[10] He was not alone in believing that education for women somehow disturbed the natural order of things and would lead to dire

73

consequences. Many scientists equated brain size with intelligence; the bigger the brain, the more intelligent the person. So-called experts argued that women who studied in college would ruin their health and their ability to have children: As their brains grew, their ovaries would shrink. The most widely read of these people was Edward Clarke, who argued in his book *Sex in Education* that the increasing numbers of white women attending college would lead to the death of the Caucasian race.

In 1885, to counter Clarke's arguments, the Association of Collegiate Alumnae, which later became the AAUW, sponsored their first national survey about the effects of education on women. They found that 78 percent of the college women they surveyed reported that they were in good health, as opposed to 50 percent of the noncollege women. The survey did little to change the minds of the men in charge of higher education, however. In 1892, Tufts University decided to discontinue its short-lived practice of admitting women, and in 1893 the women at Radcliffe (the women's division of Harvard) were told that they could use the Harvard library only after it had closed for the night and Harvard students were no longer present.

Realizing that coeducation at the nation's colleges and universities would be a long time coming, people around the country founded colleges for women modeled on the most prestigious men's institutions. In the last years of the nineteenth century, Vassar, Wellesley, Smith, Bryn Mawr, and a host of other colleges opened their doors to women only. In 1881, Sophia Packard and Harriet Giles opened Spelman College, the nation's first college for black women, in Atlanta, Georgia.

After the Civil War, women's colleges, such as Wellesley College,
began to prepare women for careers for the first time.

As the nation entered the twentieth century, most children were educated at coeducational primary and secondary schools. Those few women who went to college generally attended single-sex institutions or separate divisions of men's colleges (for example, the Radcliffe Annex of Harvard College, Pembroke College of Brown University, or Jackson College of Tufts University). They studied the same things, but using the rule that had been established for racially segregated schools, separate was considered equal.[11]

For the first fifty years of the twentieth century, this pattern continued. Although more women entered college, few went on to graduate school, and as the decade of the 1960s began, most educated women entered the fields of teaching, nursing, and secretarial work. Most expected to stop working when they married. The majority of graduate school students were male.

Women who were in their teens and twenties in post–World War II America remember overt discrimination. Speaking to Myra and David Sadker, women in their forties, fifties, and sixties recalled times during high school and college when the fact that they were female stood in the way of their education. One woman remembered, "[When I graduated from high school] in 1958 . . . only boys were allowed to take physics. It was considered inappropriate for girls." Another woman recalled taking aptitude tests in the 1950s and being told by her guidance counselor, "Well, Ann, you scored highest in the school on spatial relations, but you can forget that. There's nothing a girl can do with it." A third woman tried repeatedly between 1965 and 1968 to enroll in the industrial arts class at her high school. She

When women first began to attend college, they were accused of being unfeminine. Colleges stressed that educated women would continue to maintain their traditional skills, as is demonstrated in this World War I poster.

could not because, "The principal told me I was not allowed to take it because I was a female."[12]

There is a common thread in all of these stories: curriculum. All of these women were enrolled in coeducational schools where they were philosophically, at least, equal to the boys in their classes. Because they were girls, however, some of the courses at their schools—and some of the opportunities to which those courses could lead—were closed to them. By the 1960s, it had been two hundred years since girls had to sit outside on the steps in order to learn, but there were still important barriers to their full participation in the educational system.

## Breaking Down Barriers

The decade of the 1960s was one of significant social change. Beginning in the 1950s, black Americans had begun to resist the patterns and practices of discrimination that had restricted and threatened their lives since the first boatload of slaves arrived in 1619. During the 1960s, this civil rights movement accelerated, and by the end of the decade, other groups in the society that felt that they had not shared equally in the rewards of American democracy joined in the struggle. Among the most powerful of these groups were the feminists who led the women's movement. They looked at the way women were treated in American society and decided that economically, socially, and politically, women were not equal to men.

Education had long been a focus of the civil rights movement because education for black Americans was clearly inferior to the education available to white Americans. In spite of the landmark *Plessy* v. *Ferguson* decision, separate education for black Americans had proved not to be equal education. Far less money was spent on black schoolchildren than on white schoolchildren; the school buildings were inferior, the salaries for teachers were lower, teachers were more poorly trained, and books and equipment were often hand-me-downs from white schools.

To redress this imbalance, in the late 1960s and early 1970s, the federal government and a number of state governments passed a variety of laws that were intended to change this situation. Among the most significant of these laws were the Education Amendments of the Civil Rights Act of 1964, passed in 1972. This law was originally intended to protect people in programs receiving federal assistance or falling under federal regulations from discrimination based on race. At the last minute, the law was rewritten to include sex discrimination. Title IX added these words: "No person in the United States shall, on the basis of sex, be excluded from participation in, be denied the benefits of, or be subjected to discrimination under any education program or activity receiving Federal financial assistance."[13] Title IX was weakened by the Supreme Court in *Grove City* v. *Bell,* when the Court ruled that only programs receiving direct federal aid were subject to the regulations. However, the legislation was strengthened at the end of the 1980s, when Congress passed the Civil Rights Restoration Act of 1988, which reversed the *Grove City* decision by stating that Title IX had to be applied to all programs in any institution receiving federal funds.

By adding women to this law, the federal government signaled its willingness to end discrimination in schools. From 1972 on, it was the clear intent of the government that boys and girls would be treated equally by their schools. No longer would schools be able to prohibit girls from taking auto mechanics or boys from taking home economics. By law, girls would have to be admitted to physics and calculus classes. Colleges and universities that received government funding, which included all state institutions and the vast majority of the private ones, would have to insure equal access for men and women in all areas of the curriculum.

In the spring of 1993, a major piece of educational legislation came to the floor of the United States Congress. Called the Elementary and Secondary Education Act, this law provides federal funds to school districts for a variety of special programs. Aware of the growing research suggesting that girls are being treated unequally in many coeducational classrooms, a number of legislators proposed an amendment to the bill that would provide funding for programs designed to eliminate inequities based on gender.

Representative Patricia Schroeder, a Democrat from Colorado, joined with Patsy Mink, a Democrat from Hawaii; Dale Kildee, a Democrat from Michigan; and Olympia Snowe, a Republican from Maine, to sponsor the legislation. They called for the creation of an Office of Gender Equity at the Department of Education. This office would oversee a number of gender equity programs. Among these would be teacher training centered on gender equity, mentoring programs for women in

Representative Patricia Schroeder (center), a Democrat from
Colorado, has been instrumental in pushing for gender equity
legislation on the federal level.

mathematics and science, and school dropout prevention plans focused on teenage mothers.

This legislation put the weight of the federal government behind gender equity in schools. However, on a more local level, some school systems are now starting their own programs.

## Winning the Sports Game

Athletics had long been a part of schools' and colleges' physical education program, and it was here that the difference between the way boys and girls were treated stood out most starkly. Budgets for boys' teams were often ten to twenty times those of girls, and girls' participation in team sports was minuscule compared to that of boys. Athletics were a clear example of how boys were taught to do and girls were taught to watch. For years the image of the perfect high school couple, the prom queen and king, the Homecoming hero and heroine, had been the football captain and the cheerleader. While he went out and performed for his high school, she stood on the sidelines and cheered him on.

It was often explained that sports taught leadership, that the lessons learned on the playing field would help boys as they took their place in the business and political world. The assumption was that girls did not need this kind of leadership training because they would be on the sidelines, supporting the male leaders. Generations of schoolchildren learned to read by reading about Dick and Jane. "Run, Dick, run," read the text. "Look, Jane, look. See Dick run." Proponents of equality for women

Sports have become critical in the debate over gender equity. Under Title IX legislation, many schools and colleges have worked to make sports opportunities for boys and girls equal.

felt that this passive role for girls contributed to their lower self-esteem. They targeted athletics as one of the first areas where Title IX could make a difference.

In the years since Title IX was passed, there has been a revolution in girls' sports. In 1972, just before the passage of the act, only three-hundred-thousand high school girls played on organized athletic teams. By 1990, there were 1.8 million girls who played on interscholastic competitive teams. At the college level, the change was equally dramatic, with women's participation in sports growing by 600 percent.[14]

In spite of these numbers, however, there are still a great many inequalities in sports programs. In many areas, boys' teams still get more money, have better equipment, and attract far more attention from school administrators and fans. As one girl reported about her school, "Boys' sports teams receive much more attention and money from the school system, the student body, booster clubs, and the community. The boys' baseball team members get shoes and jackets each year and play on the best-maintained grounds. I was on the girls' softball team. We received no clothes and nobody took care of our fields. Cheerleaders did not cheer for us. We were a good team, but when we played, the bleachers were mostly empty."[15]

For girls in elementary and middle school, the answer to unequal treatment for girls' teams is often to join a boys' team. Chelsey Brodt, a young ice hockey player from Minnesota, explained, "I like playing on a boys' team because girls don't get enough ice time—only once a week. . . . The boys have ice time every day."[16] Although the unequal ice time—or field time or pool time—that Chelsey describes is common, little is done about it. Most girls will eventually have to join girls' teams as they grow older. During junior high, when girls and boys reach puberty, playing on the same team, particularly in a contact sport, becomes problematic. Boys, on average, are taller and heavier than girls after puberty. These physical differences make coeducational teams impractical, if not dangerous. Girls who have become used to playing a sport can find themselves sidelined or forced to play on an inferior team at a critical moment in the development of their self-esteem.

In spite of the growing numbers of girls in sports, boys still outnumber girls in interscholastic competition. At the high school level, about one third of all girls participate in a varsity sport, while more than half of the boys do.[17] In order for schools to prove that they have equal numbers of boys' and girls' teams, cheerleading is often counted as a varsity sport for girls. Ironically, girls' sports were once coached mostly by women, which gave girls plenty of female role models. However, after Title IX was passed, schools were forced to hire more coaches for girls' teams and to pay them on the same scale as boys' coaches. The jobs became more attractive, so more men took them. In 1972, 90 percent of the coaches for girls' teams were females. By 1990, fewer than 50 percent of the coaches for girls' teams in high school and college were women.

Leadership and role modeling are keys to changing attitudes for girls and women—or members of minority groups—in any area, so the loss of women coaches is critical. As two researchers put it, "Girls need to see many diverse women who love and participate in sport activities. . . . When they do not see this level of visibility . . . , they will likely view sport as enjoyable but unimportant or out of their realm."[18]

Sports are important, argue the proponents of girls' athletics, because team sports teach skills that lead to self-esteem. Ellen Wahl, of Girls Incorporated, an organization that acts as an advocate for girls, believes that "greater female sports participation is going to make stronger, more powerful women with a clearer sense of their capabilities."[19] A recent survey by the Women's Sports Foundation found that a significant number of women in the professional world credited their participation in sports as preparing them for the workplace by teaching them the skills needed for risk-taking and team-work. Having these skills made them more confident; confidence leads to high self-esteem. Playing sports helps people learn to be comfortable with winning as well as with losing. Luck is part of sports; no matter how hard an individual practices and plays, the team may lose. Learning to handle this disappointment and not to take it too personally is a valuable lesson. In the past, only boys were routinely exposed to the leadership lessons and confidence-building that team play can teach.

## Math and Science

Two other areas of the curriculum that have been targeted as leading areas of gender difference are mathematics and science (including the relatively new field of computer science). From the beginning of girls' education, math and science have been the subjects least likely to be stressed. They have long been thought of as hard subjects, or male subjects. When Emma Hart

Willard first opened her seminary, one of her main goals was to teach mathematics and science to girls. No girls' school in existence at the time taught these subjects. Instead, girls were taught French, sewing, dance, art, and English, subjects that were considered to be girls' subjects. Even Willard compromised, however. In order to satisfy critics who felt that biology was not a fit subject for girls, she pasted brown paper over the anatomical drawings in the biology texts that her students used.

Although schools today offer mathematics and science to all students, girls are far less likely to take courses in these subjects beyond those that meet the basic requirements for graduation from high school. Fewer still elect to major in mathematics and science in college, and there are few women in fields that are related to math and science, for example, engineering. In a 1991 survey, women were reported as being only 27 percent of mathematicians, 26 percent of statisticians, 31 percent of computer specialists, and 30 percent of biological scientists.[20]

The study of math and science is directly related to prestigious and financially rewarding careers. In our capitalist society, money means power. Scientists, engineers, doctors, accountants, dentists, computer scientists, mechanics, astronauts, statisticians, mathematics professors, chemists, and economists have careers that earn respect and high salaries. These are also professions that are dominated by men.

Researchers believe that there is a direct relationship between the way mathematics, science, and computer science are taught in most coeducational classrooms and the fact that the majority of girls choose not to study past basic levels in these areas. Researchers know that there is a direct relationship between high school and college curriculum choices and the careers that people later follow. Nationally, fewer than 15 percent of all girls take physics, while more than 25 percent of boys enroll in physics courses before they leave high school.[21] As in sports coaching, women are underrepresented in the ranks of science teachers. Less than one quarter of all high school science classes are taught by women.

Science is a hands-on field. Traditionally, American society views girls as being composed of "sugar and spice and everything nice," while boys are made of "snakes and snails and puppy dogs' tails." For Peggy Orenstein, this raises the question of "who has the right in our culture to explore the natural world, to get dirty and muddy, to think spiders and worms and frogs are neat, to bring them in for extra credit in science. In fact, to be engaged in science at all."[22] Boys do.

One of the basic themes of the AAUW study *Shortchanging Girls, Shortchanging America* was that the discomfort that girls feel about mathematics and science is directly related to self-esteem. Further, they concluded that by failing to address the high dropout rate of girls from math and science classrooms, the United States was suffering a potential loss of 50 percent of the population from technological fields that will become increasingly important in the workforce of the twenty-first century. It has been estimated that by the year 2010, the United States will lack as many as seven hundred thousand scientists and engineers. As the Sadkers have noted, "When girls self-select out of math, science and computer technology, they are making decisions that will affect the rest of their lives."[23]

It has long been a cliche that "girls just aren't good at math." In 1992, a new Teen Talk Barbie was programmed to say, "Math class is tough." The toy's inventors chose the phrase after interviewing hundreds of girls. Cliches that generalize in a disparaging way about any group in society are harmful. In a democratic society such as the United States, there is no room for ethnic or national discrimination, because the Constitution protects everyone equally. Bigoted ideas about racial, religious, or ethnic groups are legally prohibited from being used to bar members of these groups from schools, jobs, or neighborhoods. It is time that untrue, harmful generalizations about women are added to the list of characterizations that will no longer be unthinkingly accepted as barriers to their full participation in American schools and society.

# 5

# Single-Sex Education and Other Solutions

In the period of time between World War II and 1970, single-sex schools and colleges rapidly adopted coeducation because it was believed that the sexes could never achieve true equality if they were separated. Most people believed that giving boys and girls the same education would mean that they would have an equal education. Unfortunately, coeducation too often meant that women were simply additions to men's institutions. In coeducational schools and colleges, the vast majority of the classrooms, student leadership positions, and faculty are male. Men tend to dominate in coeducational environments.

In recent years, single-sex schools and colleges for girls and women have made a comeback. During the first half of the 1990s, applications to women's colleges rose by 14 percent, and the trend was almost as dramatic at

Girls who are confident and well-educated ultimately will prove to be of great value in American society.

girls' schools. Much of the research that has been described in this book has been used to prove that girls build greater self-esteem and self-confidence and experience more academic success if they are educated apart from boys. Numerous studies have shown that a disproportionate share of women who are leaders in science, politics, business, and the law are graduates of women's institutions. Cokie Roberts, an ABC News correspondent and a graduate of Wellesley College, has noted, "You really do see a lot of successful women coming out of women's colleges, particularly in journalism and politics."[1]

At an all-girls' school, girls obviously come first. They hold all the leadership positions and fill all the seats in chemistry, physics, and calculus classes. Girls' ways of learning and knowing, their sense of values, and their experiences permeate every activity every day. As one graduate of a woman's college has written, "I spent the better part of four years in a world in which women could do anything, because no one told us we couldn't."[2] A sixth grader at a girls' school in Toronto, Canada, put it this way: "There's not so much difference in what we learn as the way we learn."[3] Nor is girls' school success limited to North America. In the United Kingdom in 1994, eighteen of the schools with the top twenty results in the GCSE (national tests that are given to high school sophomores), were single-sex girls' schools.

Although many people have reported anecdotally about the feelings of self-confidence and enhanced self-esteem that graduates of girls' schools experience, until recently, there have been few solid statistics to support these claims. In a study of Catholic schools that were both coeducational and single-sex for girls and boys, researchers found that "girls' schools evidenced consistent and positive effects on student attitudes toward academics. These students were more likely to associate with academically oriented peers and to express specific interests in both mathematics and English."[4] They also concluded, "The results are particularly strong for girls' schools, where students . . . showed significantly greater gains in reading, science and educational ambition over the course of their high school years."[5]

In a statistical analysis of performance on Advanced Placement examinations, several girls' schools have found that their students score higher than would be predicted on tests in biology, English, and U.S. history. For example, at Emma Willard School, girls who take the AP biology examination are twice as likely to score above a 3 (on a scale from 1-5) as are other students whose patterns of testing on aptitude tests such as the PSAT match theirs.

Critics of girls' schools claim that an all-female environment is not the real world, and that girls who are taught in isolation from boys will not be able to deal with men in the workplace. As a sophomore at a girls' school put it, "Of course when I came here I was worried that I'd never have another date. That was silly because, of course, we do see boys socially. But the important thing to me right now is paying attention to who I am and making something of myself. I want a really good education."[6] The claims for women's colleges are indisputable. In 1992, one third of the women board members of the Fortune 1000 companies were graduates of such schools, as were 24 percent of the women in

93

Congress, and graduates of women's colleges were more than twice as likely as graduates of coeducational colleges to receive doctorate degrees. As researchers probe the experiences of girls in high schools, it appears likely that the statistics will be equally impressive. In the meantime, testimonies to the impact of girls' schools on women's feelings of self-esteem abound. As Kathleen Odean, an editor of *Glamour*, put it, "At my all-girls' school, I developed a voice. That all-female environment offered me some time to build up strength before entering a world where men's voices command more attention than women's."

## Single-Sex Classes

Most girls do not have access to all-girls' schools. Although a few public schools remain single-sex schools (for example, Girls' High School in Philadelphia), the vast majority of single-sex schools are private and independent. Since these schools have selective admissions standards and are typically very expensive, they are able to serve the needs of only a small, mostly affluent percentage of the millions of girls who attend school.

On the local level, some school administrators recently have begun experimenting with gender-segregated classrooms in some subjects, typically mathematics and science. In Ventura, California, for instance, two high schools have experimented with separate classes in Algebra II and chemistry. Some of the plan's critics have charged that teaching girls separately may lead people to think that girls are weak and need to be coddled. Girls who are participating in the segregated classrooms, however, like the experience and claim that they have greater opportunity to learn without boys present. One girl told a reporter, "Math was my worst subject, and now it's turned out to be pretty fun." Another girl likes the all-girls' atmosphere because "You don't have to hide a part of your personality and pretend you're confused when you know what's happening."[7] At the Illinois Math and Science Academy, another school that is experimenting with segregated classrooms, a student in an all-girls' science class spoke proudly of the "physics freedom" that she and her female classmates had earned.[8]

A junior high school in Manassas, Virginia, is the first public school in that state to experiment with all-girl classes. In 1995, one hundred students in the eighth grade were segregated by sex in some of their courses, especially mathematics and science classes. Some people, including Rosemary Dempsey, vice president of the National Organization for Women, think that it is wrong for a public school to separate students on the basis of sex. She told a reporter, "Instead of getting to the root of the problem, this is sending the message to boys and girls that they're the problem. It's saying there's something unequal about girls and they can't do well in an integrated society or classroom."[9] However, the girls in the program have been immensely complimentary about its effects on their work. One of them remembered that in her former coed math class, "If I answered a question wrong, guys would make fun of me. . . . If I didn't understand something or if I was having trouble, I wouldn't ask questions . . . I'd go home without understanding it."[10]

Although it is too early to have concrete statistical

support for the experiments in Ventura and Manassas, the girls' experiences point in the direction of success. Amy, another student in Virginia, pointed out that her grades jumped from Ds to As and that she now plans to become a doctor, a career she believed was impossible before: "I used to think I was a math moron. I thought I'd have to look for a career with as little math as possible."[11] If segregated classrooms in the middle school years encourage more girls to take math and science and to strive for careers in fields that use these disciplines, they will have been successful. At the same time, their success illustrates the failure of coeducational classrooms to support these talents and interests in girls.

## Making Changes in Your School

Your school probably is coeducational. If you are a girl, you most likely have experienced some of the gender bias described in this book. You may not have recognized it as such, and you may not have known what, if anything, you could do about it. There are some things you can do about it. First, you need to ask to meet with the teachers or coaches where you think the inequity is occurring. In most cases, they will probably be unaware that they have been giving some members of the classroom more attention. Female teachers may be more receptive to your suggestions because they may have experienced some of the same things while they were in school. Most male teachers will be eager to change as well. If you meet resistance, try arranging a meeting with the principal or another school administrator to discuss your concerns. If you still are not getting a response, enlist your parents' support.

Change, particularly when it involves correcting patterns of behavior that have been established over a very long period of time, can be very difficult. The person who speaks out against injustice can often feel isolated and alone. Try to enlist the support of your good friends, both girls and boys, so that there is a small group of you who can provide each other with support. Together you may make a difference.

## "Sweetest Personality"

In a kindergarten graduation ceremony in June 1994, awards were given out to the five- and six-year-olds who were heading to first grade. Awards went to girls for having the "sweetest personality" and to boys for being the "very best thinker." A girl received a prize for being the "best artist," and a boy for being the "most scientific."[12] For these very young children—and for too many other children all over the country and the world—the gender patterns reflected in these awards will be reinforced throughout their education. Until we recognize and stop this kind of stereotyping, girls will continue to lose out in society, and society will lose as well.

# Helpful Organizations

Often teachers are very willing to change, but do not know about books or strategies that will help correct inequities in the classroom. You can tell them about organizations that have worked to design gender-balanced curricula, produce gender-balanced bibliographies of textbooks, and host workshops that will help teachers recognize and change classroom patterns that lead to inequity. Among them are:

**American Association of University Women**
1111 16th Street N.W.
Washington, D.C. 20036
202-785-7700

**Center for Research on Women**
Wellesley College
106 Central Street
Wellesley, MA 02181
617-283-2500

**Consortium for Educational Equity**
Rutgers University
Bldg. 4090 Livingston Campus
New Brunswick, NJ 08903
908-445-2071

### Educational Equity Concepts
114 E. 32nd Street, Suite 701
New York, NY 10016
212-725-1803

### Gender Equity Center of Western Massachusetts
Springfield Technical Community College
Bldg. 16, Room 147
Springfield, MA 01105
413-781-7822

### Girls Count
225 East 16th Ave., Suite 475
Denver, CO 80203
303-832-6600

### Girls Incorporated
National Resource Center
441 West Michigan Street
Indianapolis, MN 46202-3233
800-374-4475
*also:*
Girls Incorporated
30 East 33rd Street, 7th Floor
New York, NY 10016
(212) 689-3700

### National Association for Women in Education
1325 18th Street N.W., Suite 210
Washington, DC 20036
202-659-9330

**The National Coalition of Girls' Schools**
228 Main Street
Concord, MA 01742
508-287-4485

**National Women's Studies Association**
University of Maryland
7100 Baltimore Ave., Suite 301
College Park, MD 20740
301-403-0525

***New Moon* Magazine**
**By, for and about girls.**
P.O. Box 3587
Duluth, MN  55803
1-800-381-4743

**Women and Mathematics Education**
SummerMath
Mount Holyoke College
50 College Street
South Hadley, MA 01075-1441
413-538-2608

**Women's College Coalition**
125 Michigan Avenue N.E.
Washington, D.C. 20017
202-234-0443

**Women's Educational Act Publishing Center**
55 Chapel Street
Newton, MA 02158
617-969-7100

## Women's Educational Equity Act Resource Center
Educational Development Center
55 Chapel Street
Newton, MA 02158-1060
800-225-3088

# Chapter Notes

## Chapter 1

1. It is important to recognize that self-esteem varies among girls from different backgrounds. Latina girls, for example, suffer greater loss of self-esteem than white girls, while African-American girls suffer the least loss of self-esteem. These patterns are documented in the American Association of University Women surveys and in the work of Peggy Orenstein, both of which are cited below.

2. Peggy Orenstein, *School Girls: Young Women, Self-Esteem & the Confidence Gap,* (New York: Doubleday & Company, 1994), p. xv.

3. American Association of University Women, *Shortchanging Girls, Shortchanging America,* (Washington, D.C.: American Association of University Women Foundation, 1991), p. 5.

## Chapter 2

1. Myra Sadker and David M. Sadker, *Failing at Fairness: How America's Schools Cheat Girls,* (New York: Macmillan Publishing Co., 1994), p. 93.

2. Ibid.

3. Myra Sadker and David M. Sadker, "Why Schools

Must Tell Girls: You're Smart, You Can Do It," *USA Weekend,* February 4–6, 1994, p. 4.

4. Quoted in Charles S. Clark, "Education and Gender," *CQ Researcher,* June 3, 1994, p. 483.

5. Judy Mann, *The Difference: Growing Up Female in America,* (New York: Warner Books, 1994), p. 160.

6. Margie, "Three Girls and Their Bunsen Burners," *Sassy,* September 1994, p. 95.

7. Peggy Orenstein, *School Girls: Young Women, Self-Esteem & the Confidence Gap,* (New York: Doubleday & Company, 1994), p. xix.

8. Ibid., pp. 100–101.

9. Myra Sadker et al., "Gender Equity in the Classroom: The Unfinished Agenda," *The College Board Review,* Winter 1993–94, p. 14.

10. Orenstein, p. 300.

11. "Schoolyard Teasing Now Has a New Name," *CQ Researcher,* June 3, 1994, p. 494.

12. Ibid., p. 495.

13. Quoted in Orenstein, p. 129.

14. Tamar Lewin, "Students Seeking Damages for Sex Bias," *New York Times,* July 15, 1994, p. B7.

15. Ibid., p. B8.

16. Sadker and Sadker, *Failing at Fairness,* p. viii.

17. Charisse Jones, "Test Scores Show Gaps by Ethnicity," *New York Times,* July 8, 1994, p. B3.

18. Ibid.

19. Sadker and Sadker, *Failing at Fairness,* p. 136.

20. Ibid., p. 140.

21. Orenstein, p. xiv.

## Chapter 3

1. Carol Gilligan, "Woman's Place in Man's Life Cycle," *Harvard Educational Review,* Winter 1980.

2. Carol Gilligan, Nona P. Lyons, and Trudy J. Hanmer, eds., *Making Connections: The Relational Worlds of Adolescent Girls at Emma Willard School,* (Troy, N. Y.: Emma Willard School, 1989).

3. Quoted in *Making Connections,* p. 53.

4. Ibid., p. 38.

5. Ibid., p. 50.

6. Letter from Lyn Mikel Brown to Jane Steltenpohl, editor, Enslow Publishers, Inc., March 14, 1995.

7. Ibid.

8. L. Kim, "Boys Will Be Boys . . . Right?" *The Lance,* Livingston High School (N.J.), June 1993, p. 5.

9. Myra Sadker and David M. Sadker, "Sexism in the Schoolroom of the '80s," *Psychology Today,* March 1985, p. 3.

10. Myra Sadker and David M. Sadker, *Failing at*

*Fairness: How America's Schools Cheat Girls,* (New York: Macmillan Publishing Co., 1994), p. ix.

11. Ibid., p. 76.

12. Ibid., p. 55.

13. Ibid., p. 156.

14. Peggy Orenstein, *School Girls: Young Women, Self-Esteem & the Confidence Gap,* (New York: Doubleday & Company, 1994), p. 20.

15. Judy Mann, *The Difference: Growing Up Female in America,* (New York: Warner Books, 1994), p. 82.

16. Bernice R. Sandler and Roberta M. Hall, *The Classroom Climate: A Chilly One for Women,* (Washington, D.C.: Association of American Colleges, 1982), p. 1.

17. American Association of University Women, *How Schools Shortchange Girls,* (Washington, D.C.: American Association of University Women Foundation, 1992), p. 67.

18. Quoted in *How Schools Shortchange Girls,* p. 67.

## Chapter 4

1. Myra Sadker and David M. Sadker, *Failing at Fairness: How America's Schools Cheat Girls,* (New York: Macmillan Publishing Co., 1994), p. 25.

2. Elaine Kendall, "Beyond Mother's Knee," *American Heritage,* June 1973, p. 13.

3. Ibid., p. 14.

4. Ibid.

5. The Troy Female Seminary was renamed Emma Willard School after its founder, and remains a college-preparatory all-girls' high school today.

6. Emma Willard, *A Plan for Improving Female Education,* reprint, (Marietta, Ga.: Larlin Corporation, 1987), p. 19.

7. Ibid., p. 8.

8. Quoted in Sadker and Sadker, p. 18.

9. Elisabeth Griffith, *In Her Own Right: The Life of Elizabeth Cady Stanton,* (New York: Oxford University Press, 1984), p. 202.

10. Lynn Dorothy Gordon, *Gender & Higher Education in the Progressive Era,* (New Haven, Conn.: Yale University Press, 1990), p. 22.

11. In the Supreme Court case *Plessy* v. *Ferguson,* the Supreme Court ruled in 1893 that segregation was constitutional as long as the schools provided for black and white children were equal.

12. Sadker and Sadker, pp. 33–34.

13. Quoted in Connie M. Thorngren and Barbara S. Eisenbarth, "Games Yet to Be Played: Equity in Sport Leadership," *Women's Educational Equity Act Publishing Center Digest,* June 1994, p. 1.

14. Sadker and Sadker, p. 125.

15. Ibid., p. 127.

16. Brooks Whitney, "She Shoots, She Scores," *American Girl,* January/February 1995, p. 24.

17. Mary C. Hickey, "How Girls Win Self-Esteem," *Working Mother,* January 1994, p. 51.

18. Thorngren and Eisenbarth, p. 2.

19. Hickey, p. 50.

20. Dory Adams, "Women + Science + Math = ?" *NAIS/CWIS Newsnotes,* Spring 1991, p. 1.

21. Ibid.

22. Peggy Orenstein, *School Girls: Young Women, Self-Esteem & the Confidence Gap,* (New York: Doubleday & Company, 1994), p. 22.

23. Sadker and Sadker, p. 125.

## Chapter 5

1. Women's College Coalition pamphlet, Washington, D.C., 1994, p. 17.

2. Susan Estrich, "Separate Is Better," *New York Times,* May 22, 1994, p. 39.

3. Andrew Duffy, "More Same Sex Schools Urged," *Toronto Star,* December 7, 1993, p. 12.

4. Valaris E. Lee and Anthony S. Bryk, *Effects of Single-Sex Secondary Schools on Student Achievement and Attitudes,* (Washington, D.C.: American Psychological Association, 1986), p. 387.

5. Ibid., p. 394.

6. "How Best to Prepare Girls to Excel in the Real World," (Troy, N.Y.: Emma Willard School, 1993), p. 13.

7. Jane Gross, "All-Girl Classes to Help Girls Keep Up With Boys," *New York Times,* November 24, 1993, p. B8.

8. Estrich, p. 39.

9. Eric L. Wee, "A Lesson in Confidence," *Washington Post,* May 1, 1995, p. A1.

10. Ibid.

11. Ibid., p. A13.

12. Kathleen Deveny, "Chart of Kindergarten Awards," *Wall Street Journal,* December 5, 1994.

# Bibliography

American Association of University Women. *How Schools Shortchange Girls.* Washington, D.C.: American Association of University Women Foundation, 1992.

————*Shortchanging Girls, Shortchanging America.* Washington, D.C.: American Association of University Women Foundation, 1991.

Brown, Lyn Mikel, and Carol Gilligan. *Meeting at the Crossroads: Women's Psychology and Girls' Development.* Cambridge, Mass.: Harvard University Press, 1992.

Gilligan, Carol, Nona P. Lyons, and Trudy J. Hanmer, eds., *Making Connections: The Relational Worlds of Girls at Emma Willard School.* Troy, NY: Emma Willard School, 1989.

Gordon, Lynn Dorothy. *Gender and Higher Education in the Progressive Era.* New Haven, Conn.: Yale University Press, 1990.

Griffith, Elisabeth. *In Her Own Right: The Life of Elizabeth Cady Stanton.* New York: Oxford University Press, 1984.

Mann, Judy. *The Difference: Growing Up Female in America.* New York: Warner Books, 1994.

Orenstein, Peggy. *School Girls: Young Women, Self-Esteem & the Confidence Gap.* New York: Doubleday & Company, 1994.

Sadker, Myra, and David M. Sadker. *Failing at Fairness: How America's Schools Cheat Girls.* New York: Macmillan Publishing Co., 1994.

Sandler, Bernice R., and Roberta M. Hall. *The Classroom Climate: A Chilly One for Women.* Washington, D.C.: Association of American Colleges, 1982.

# Index